"This is a brilliant combination of analysis and prescription. Andy Serwer describes the disruptions of the past decade, why they happened, and how we can bounce back. The result is forward-looking history at its most valuable."

—WALTER ISAACSON
Author of *Einstein* and *American Sketches*

"Andy Serwer's *Starting Over* is an important first draft of history that gives readers badly needed perspective on a tragic confluence of events that savaged our economy, stretched our military, and weakened America's standing in the world."

—JOE SCARBOROUGH
Host of MSNBC's *Morning Joe* and author of *The Last Best Hope*

"Business leaders must understand how the world has changed in the last decade and what lies ahead in the next. This book is a must-read for anyone wanting to develop a new perspective."

—RAM CHARAN
Author and adviser to *Fortune* Global 500 executives

Starting Over

WHY THE LAST DECADE WAS SO
DAMN ROTTEN AND WHY THE NEXT
ONE WILL SURELY BE BETTER

ANDY SERWER

MANAGING EDITOR OF FORTUNE MAGAZINE

TIME Books

ISBN 10: 1-60320-160-2
ISBN 13: 978-1-60320-160-5
Library of Congress Control Number: 2009943079

We welcome your comments and suggestions
about Time Books. Please write to us at:

Time Books
Attention: Book Editors
PO Box 11016
Des Moines, Iowa 50336-1016

If you would like to order any of our hardcover Collector's Edition books,
please call us at 1-800-327-6388 (Monday through Friday, 7 a.m. to 8 p.m.,
or Saturday, 7 a.m. to 6 p.m., Central Time).

To my daughters, Emily and Kate

Author's Note

I was well aware of the great "When does the decade begin?" controversy when I started this piece. (Some say the decade ends Dec. 31, 1999; others, the end of 2000.) I remembered this argument from the days of Y2K. In fact, that's what made me come down on the 2009 side of the debate. Back then it seemed as if most folks considered the last decade over on Dec. 31, 1999. So I thought that it made sense to use that benchmark for this decade as well. The editors at *Time* agreed with me, and given the name of their magazine, maybe they deserve a little license.

Table of Contents

Measuring Up

WE MEASURE OUR LIVES—AND OUR NATIONAL LIFE— in decades. But of course there's nothing natural about a decade—the universe couldn't care less about 10-year increments. We care because it's a way of framing our own history—an artificial creation that orders the past. Decades may measure time, but they are first and foremost psychic measurements.

When I mention the Sixties or the Eighties, you will see an instant movie in your head of what was going on in our national life and in your own. You might hear the opening chords of a Beatles song, see an image of Ronald Reagan, or recall some black-and-white pictures from your high school yearbook.

One simple problem with the decade that we just came through is that it never found its name. The '00s? The aughts? Nothing stuck. When Andy came to me in October of 2009 and said, "You know, no one realizes the decade is coming to an end, and no one has yet named it," I thought, I want *Time* to do that story. Andy's piece became a memorable cover story called "The Decade From Hell" and furnished the basis for this book.

As we were doing the story, someone said to me, "I don't want to name the '00s. I just want to forget them." But as far as I'm concerned, Andy named the decade, and we would do well not to forget the Decade From Hell. A lot of lessons can be learned from the past 10 years. They began with 9/11, ended with the financial meltdown, and had Katrina in the middle. They also had Saddam Hussein, the invasion of Afghanistan, Abu Ghraib, the tsunami in Southeast Asia, and Bernie Madoff. Sorry to depress you. I know lots of good things happened in the '00s too. People fell in love, adorable babies were born, great art and literature were created. Our private lives and the world of events do not run parallel, but they do intersect. A falling tide takes every boat down a couple of inches.

The enduring message in what Andy writes is that we are not doomed to repeat the mistakes of the past 10 years. Katrina was both a natural disaster and a man-made one: The storm was an act of God, but building the levees too low was due to our own very human shortsightedness. Structured investment vehicles and credit default swaps are not found in nature: We made them ourselves to finance McMansions and yachts. We knew of al Qaeda long before two jets crashed into the Twin Towers.

I know I began by saying there's nothing natural about decades, and there isn't. But because we place so much emphasis on them, they often become a kind of pendulum. Each decade becomes a reaction to the previous one. I'm hopeful that the next decade will avoid the excesses of the one we've just come out of. So get ready for the Teens—the Decade of Responsibility.

—*Richard Stengel*
MANAGING EDITOR OF *TIME* MAGAZINE

2000

Nasdaq peaks at 5049, Dow at 11,723. **Torrential rains and flooding leave more than a million homeless in Africa.** Bridgestone/Firestone recalls 6.5 million tires. **Price of gasoline nears $2 a gallon.** Federal agents remove Elián González from relatives' home in Miami. **Air France Concorde crash kills 113.** Israel's soon-to-be Prime Minister, Ariel Sharon, visits the Temple Mount, sparking Palestinian *intifadeh*. **Al Qaeda suicide bombers strike the U.S.S.** ***Cole*, killing 17 sailors.** Retailer Montgomery Ward closes after 128 years. **U.S. presidential election ends in chaos and is resolved by the Supreme Court.**

2001

George W. Bush is inaugurated after disputed court ruling. **Washington is gripped by disappearance of Hill intern Chandra Levy.** U.S. economy goes into recession. **Nineteen Islamic terrorists fly hijacked jets into the World Trade Center and the Pentagon, killing nearly 3,000.** Anthrax-contaminated letters are mailed to news organizations and U.S. Senate offices, killing five and setting off panic. **U.S. invades Afghanistan.** American Airlines Flight 587 crashes in Queens, N.Y., killing 265. **Enron files for Chapter 11, the largest bankruptcy in U.S. history to date.**

2002

Turncoat John Walker Lindh gets 20 years for fighting for the Taliban. **U.S. introduces color-coded threat alerts.** Beltway snipers strike, killing at least 10 people in the D.C. area. **Reporter Daniel Pearl (left) is kidnapped and murdered in Pakistan.** The Pope and Vatican officials acknowledge priest sexual-abuse scandal. **Air-show disaster in Ukraine kills 83.** Bombings at nightclubs in Bali, Indonesia, kill about 200. **Congress authorizes U.S. military action against Iraq.** Chechen terrorists seize Moscow theater; some 120 hostages die during rescue operation by Russian forces. **WorldCom discloses accounting fraud, declares bankruptcy.**

2003

Space shuttle *Columbia* disintegrates during reentry; seven die. **Power failure blacks out millions in U.S. and Canada.** U.S. begins invasion of Iraq by bombing Baghdad. **Fire at nightclub in Rhode Island kills 100.** Record number of tornadoes during one week: 393 in 19 states. **President Bush declares "Mission accomplished" as insurgency grows in Iraq.** Martha Stewart is indicted in insider-trading case. **CIA officer Valerie Plame's cover is blown by columnist.** White House admits faulty intelligence on Iraq's WMD. **Earthquake in Iran kills more than 26,000.** Mad-cow disease reaches U.S. **World Health Organization issues alert on SARS.**

2004

U.S. death toll in Iraq passes 1,000. **Photos of prisoner abuse by guards at Abu Ghraib are made public.** President Bush is reelected, defeating Democratic Senator John Kerry. **Islamic terrorists attack trains in Madrid, killing nearly 200.** Scott Peterson is charged with murdering his pregnant wife. **Tests confirm dioxin poisoning of Ukrainian presidential candidate Viktor Yushchenko.** Chechen terrorists take 1,000-plus hostages at North Ossetian school; more than 300 are killed. **Tsunami kills more than 200,000 people in about a dozen countries in Southeast Asia and Africa.**

2005

Mahmoud Ahmadinejad wins Iranian presidential election. **North Korea says it has nuclear weapons.** House Majority Leader Tom DeLay is indicted for violating election laws. **U.S. military death toll in Iraq tops 2,000.** Hurricane Katrina strikes New Orleans; levees break; more than 1,500 are killed. **Homegrown suicide bombers strike London transit system, killing more than 50.** Indonesia reports its first case of bird flu in humans; the disease reaches Europe and Africa the following year. **Earthquake in Kashmir kills some 80,000.** Disaffected youths from immigrant communities in Paris suburbs start riots that plague France for weeks.

2006

Lobbyist Jack Abramoff pleads guilty to conspiracy to bribe lawmakers. **Charles Carl Roberts IV kills five girls at a Pennsylvania Amish school, then himself, in one of three school shootings in a week.** Former Enron chiefs Ken Lay and Jeffrey Skilling are found guilty of fraud. **Gas tops $3 a gallon.** Mini-war between Israel and Hezbollah kills 1,007 in Lebanon. **S&P/Case-Shiller home price index peaks; housing bubble starts to burst.** Defense Secretary Donald Rumsfeld resigns after Republicans lose majority in Congress. **Saddam Hussein is executed by hanging.** American military deaths in Iraq reach 3,000.

2007

Report on steroid use in baseball is issued; 89 players implicated. **UN panel says evidence of global warming is "unequivocal."** Southern California wildfires force evacuations, destroy more than 2,000 homes. **Decline in Chinese market triggers global market crash.** Former Pakistani Prime Minister Benazir Bhutto is assassinated by al Qaeda. **Student at Virginia Tech guns down 32, then himself.** Highway bridge in Minneapolis collapses, killing 13. **Senator Larry Craig pleads guilty to disorderly conduct after airport-bathroom gay-sex sting.** Federal Reserve chairman Ben Bernanke warns that economy will worsen.

2008

Death toll for U.S. troops in Iraq reaches 4,000. **Law-enforcement officials raid ranch of polygamist sect in Texas.** Wenchuan earthquake in China leaves 80,000 dead or missing. **Oil hits record $147 a barrel.** U.S. government takes control of Fannie Mae and Freddie Mac. **Lehman files for bankruptcy; stock markets plunge.** Barack Obama is elected President. **Illinois Governor Rod Blagojevich is charged in plot to sell Obama's vacant Senate seat.** Terrorist attacks in Mumbai kill more than 170 people. **Dow drops nearly 34% for the year, the worst decline since 1931; S&P is down 38.5%, its worst year since 1937.**

2009

Chrysler and General Motors declare bankruptcy; the government becomes part-owner. **President Obama announces $275 billion plan to prevent foreclosures.** US Airways flight makes "miracle" landing on Hudson River after bird strike; no fatalities. **Bernie Madoff pleads guilty to fraud equal to an estimated $65 billion.** Obama signs $787 billion stimulus package. **Ahmadinejad is declared winner of Iranian election; violent protests in the streets.** Proposed U.S. budget is $3.6 trillion, with 2009 deficit projected at $1.75 trillion. **World Health Organization says H1N1 flu is a global pandemic.** Unemployment rate hits 10.2%.

Starting Over

I.

In the Beginning

AT EXACTLY TWO MINUTES AFTER MIDNIGHT ON JAN. 1, 2000, an alarm sounded at a nuclear power plant in Onagawa, Japan. Government officials and computer scientists around the globe held their breath. Was this the beginning of a massive Y2K computer meltdown? Actually, no. It was an isolated event, one of a handful of glitches to occur (including the failure of 500 slot machines at two racetracks in Delaware) as the sun rose on the new decade. The dreaded millennial meltdown never happened.

World Trade Center, 9/11/2001 *The Decade From Hell begins: Al Qaeda terrorists crash hijacked airliners into the Twin Towers.*

Instead, it was the American Dream that was about to dim. Bookended by 9/11 at the start and a financial wipeout at the end, the first 10 years of this century will very likely go down as the most dispiriting and disillusioning decade that Americans have lived through in the post–World War II era. Maybe we should have known something was amiss when the pundits were stumped trying to give the decade a name. Some wanted the "uh-ohs," others the "aughts," while the popular historian Niall Ferguson uses the term "noughties." Apt, but something a bit less cutesy would be better. The Decade From Hell, or the Reckoning, or the Decade of Broken Dreams, or the Lost Decade—they all seem more appropriate. Call it whatever you want; just give thanks that it is over.

Calling the 2000s "the worst" may seem an overwrought label, in historical terms, for a decade in which we fought no major wars. It is a sadly appropriate term for the families of the thousands of 9/11 victims and soldiers and others killed in Iraq and Afghanistan. But the lack of a large-scale armed conflict makes these past 10 years stand out that much more. This decade was as awful as any peacetime decade in the nation's entire history. Between the West's ongoing struggle against radical Islam and our recent near-death economic experience—trends that have largely skirted much of the developing world—it's no wonder we feel as if we've been through a 10-year gauntlet. Americans may have the darkest view of recent history, since it's in the U.S. that the effects of those trends have been most acute.

To be sure, some historians will tell you that this decade really wasn't so bad. "People assume their problems are unique. It's a lack of historical perspective," Ferguson says, citing the decades of the 1930s, 1940s, and 1980s as having been worse for the world economy. "Our standard of living is higher on average than anytime in history." Depending on how you measure, Ferguson is partially right, particularly if you are from, say, China or Brazil. If you live there or in other parts of the developing world, you may have had a pretty good decade economically. As for the U.S., once it was the sunniest and most optimistic of nations. No longer.

The U.S. has endured not one but two market crashes —one at each end of the decade. You might recall the first

Wall Street crash, when swooning tech stocks tanked the market from 2000 to 2001, not long after the Nasdaq hit an all-time high of 5049 on March 10, 2000. The economy went into a recession that now seems laughably mild. What followed wasn't funny at all: the most divisive and confusing presidential election in history, a discombobulated drama that we once thought could occur only in the Third World.

Then came the defining moment of the decade, the terrorist attacks of 9/11, which redefined global politics for at least a generation. We waged a war in Afghanistan that drags on today and is deadlier than ever. Then came our fiasco in Iraq. Don't forget the anthrax letters, and later the Washington, D.C., snipers, or the wave of Wall Street scandals exemplified by Enron and WorldCom.

Sometimes it was as if the gods themselves were conspiring against this decade. On Aug. 29, 2005, Hurricane Katrina made landfall in southeastern Louisiana, killing more than 1,500 and causing $100 billion in damage. It was the largest natural disaster in our nation's history.

There is nothing natural about the economic meltdown we are still struggling with. A housing bubble fueled by cheap money and excessive borrowing set ablaze by derivatives put the economy on the brink of collapse. We will be sorting through the wreckage for years. Meanwhile the living, breathing symbol of this economic sordidness—prisoner No. 61727-054, a.k.a. Bernie Madoff—rots away in a Butner, N.C., jail cell, doing 150 years for orchestrating the biggest Ponzi scheme in the history of humanity.

I should acknowledge what some might say is a glaring error in my argument. I was well aware of the great "When does the decade begin?" controversy when I started to write a cover story for *Time* magazine, "The Decade From Hell"—the piece from which this book originated. Some say the previous decade ended Dec. 31, 1999; others, the end of 2000. I remembered this argument from the days of Y2K. In fact, that's what made me come down on the 2009 side of the debate. Back then it seemed as if most folks considered the last decade over on Dec. 31, 1999. So I thought it made sense to use that benchmark for this decade as well. The editors here agreed with me, and given that the name of the magazine is *Time*, maybe they deserve a little license.

II

The Great Meltdown

WERE WE AMERICANS ALONE IN OUR TROUBLES?
Hardly. The Asian tsunami of 2004 killed more than
200,000 people. And our financial meltdown quickly
spread around the developed world. Yet from our lofty
perch overlooking the 20th century—the American Century, as *Time*'s co-founder once labeled it—the fall has
been precipitous. Who among us is unscathed? Not
many. Even if none of your family members died in
combat, if you had no money with Madoff, and if you

New York Stock Exchange, March 2008 *The collapse of Bear Stearns's
stock was prelude to the subprime-mortgage meltdown on Wall Street.*

own your house free and clear, you most likely still took a hit. To paraphrase the question Ronald Reagan posed years ago, Are you better off today than you were at the beginning of the decade? For most of us, the answer is a resounding no.

Recall that the decade began with great promise. With Y2K out of the way, most of us kept on partying like it was 1999 in those waning days of the Clinton presidency. Wall Street continued to boom. And why not? On Jan. 4, 2000, Alan Greenspan was nominated for a fourth term as head of the Federal Reserve. On Jan. 10, AOL announced its ill-fated and over-the-top deal to buy Time Warner (parent company of this book's publisher)—at $147 billion, the biggest merger in U.S. history. Four days later the Dow hit 11,723. The Nasdaq topped out on March 10. It was pretty much all downhill after that.

The pain was delivered in myriad ways. For one thing, the stock market is down 26%* since 2000. (Inflation-adjusted, it's even worse.) In fact, the only other time in the past 100 years that stocks declined over the entire decade was the 1930s. Incidentally, I remember Warren

*All figures as of Nov. 24, 2009.

Buffett telling me at the beginning of the decade that there was no way the go-go returns of the 1990s were going to continue, and that we had better get used to meager returns going forward. Buffett saw it coming.

For the average working stiff it was a pretty lousy 10 years. The median household income in 2000 was $52,500. In 2008 (the most recent year available) it was $50,303. And given that the unemployment rate has climbed to 10.2%, income will almost certainly drop again this year. Low-income Americans fared even worse. In 2000, 11.3% of Americans were living below the poverty line. By 2008 that number had risen to 13.2%. Meanwhile, the percentage of Americans without health insurance increased from 13.7% to 15.4%.

Surprisingly, housing prices were not such a debacle—that is, if you bought early and stayed put. The median price of an existing home was $143,600 in 2000. Today the median is nearly $175,000. But remember, millions of Americans splurged for homes in the middle of the decade when prices were high: In July 2006 the median selling price peaked at $230,300. If you bought then—assuming you haven't lost your house to

foreclosure—your home has lost some 25% of its value. Nothing to cheer about there.

Our national psyche has been damaged as much as our national economy by the record number of corporate bankruptcies, many of them household names: Kmart, United Airlines, Circuit City, Lehman Brothers, GM, and Chrysler. Major bankruptcies such as these have a ripple effect: Thousands of jobs are lost. Suppliers lose huge chunks of business. Crimped companies cut back on quality. Housing prices decline. Tax rolls fall. Municipalities suffer, and the quality of life diminishes.

The price of oil more than tripled this decade, settling at over $70 a barrel, which acted like a tax on our economy. Here, too, we had been living beyond our means. For years the price of gasoline climbed slower than general inflation, giving us an illusion of wealth. We were in denial that this was an unsustainable advantage and splurged on SUVs and bought mega-homes miles and miles away from our jobs and lacked any public transportation to connect the two. Oil prices aren't likely to decline to low or medium double digits anytime soon.

(If they didn't during the recent catastrophic recession, when would they?) This reckoning has hit U.S. automakers and airline companies—not to mention consumers—like a kick in the gut.

Of course, the decade's bad news hasn't been confined to the financial pages. Was there actually more bad news than usual? Leaving aside the tragic litany of plane crashes, earthquakes, and typhoons that occur randomly every 10 years, the answer is an objective yes. For example, there were more mass shootings and school shootings, such as the murder of 32 students at Virginia Tech in 2007 and the 2009 slaughter at Fort Hood, than in any other decade. There were more large-scale terrorist bombings and attacks in countries like England, Spain, Pakistan, Indonesia, Russia, Jordan, the Philippines, Turkey, India, and, of course, the U.S. The absolute number killed was not great, but the idea that terrorists can attack anytime and anywhere is new and profoundly unsettling.

Even many of our heroes turned out to be badly flawed, from the doping by athletes in baseball, cycling, and the Olympics to the endless political scandals and sex scandals. And yes, we couldn't get enough of them on the 24-hour cable news, blogs, and reality TV that chronicled and reflected this unsavory display. (White House gatecrashers, anyone?) The rise of all manner of new media and the lack of barriers to criticism from the blogosphere seemed to intensify every scandal and left very few public figures unsullied. Sure, some amazingly great things happened this decade, from the stunning rise of China, to Apple's dazzling array of new products, to the feats of sprinter Usain Bolt, to our nation's rallying (at least temporarily) around its first African-American President. But all that seems more like a sideshow rather than the main act.

The rise of technology played a role too. Only a Luddite would suggest that technology was "evil" per se and needed to be reversed. But it is true that technological know-how has increased faster than our ability to understand its implications or control its effects. Consider our inability to safeguard the world's strategic weapons, or the ease with which al Qaeda, or for that matter a mass murderer armed to the teeth, acts. Consider, too, our lack of controls over derivatives—"financial weapons of mass destruction," in the words of Warren Buffett, who has expressed concern about this general point. These complex, computer-driven financial instruments nearly took out the global economy recently. We are so talented at creating breakthrough technologies, but less talented at understanding their unintended consequences.

Perhaps we were lulled into complacency by the exuberance of the end of the Cold War. It was a deception brought on by an unusually positive historical continuum. First, America and the Allies won World War II; then, 45 years later, with the fall of the Berlin Wall, we defeated communism too. After that, maybe we believed the world would be forever free of conflict. Some thinkers called it the end of history. Well, history did not die. It came roaring back. The old conflicts did indeed wither, but new and virulent ones arose.

III.
What Went Wrong

SO HERE'S THE BIG QUESTION: WHY? WHY DID SO MUCH bad stuff happen in this decade? Was it just rotten luck, or something more? Sure, some of it was simply randomness, but I think a strong case can be made that it was more than just chance that got things so bollixed up.

First, a note on partisan politics. After *Time* published "The Decade From Hell," the editors immediately received a large number of letters laying the blame for the ills of this decade at the feet of President George

War zone *In November 2009, a soldier from the 82nd Airborne patrols Afghanistan's Zabul province, a transit hub for Taliban militants.*

W. Bush. After all, they pointed out, he was President 80% of the time. It's an easy finger to point if you are a liberal or a Democrat, and to be perfectly objective, there is merit to the argument, especially considering that much of the decade is defined by our forays into Iraq and Afghanistan, lax oversight of the financial markets, and the inept public response to Katrina. They are huge lapses, and the President and his men are directly responsible for those actions and their terrible effects. Yet the real problems of the decade stem from far deeper sources than simply some ill-conceived neoconservative dreams.

In large part, we have ourselves to blame. If you look at the underlying causes of some of the most troubling developments of the decade, you can see striking common denominators. The raft of financial problems, our war with radical Islam, the collapse of GM and much of our domestic auto industry, and even the devastation brought about by Katrina all came about at least in part or were greatly exacerbated by:

Neglect. Our inward-looking culture didn't heed the warning signs from around the world—and from within our own country—that Islamic terrorism was heading for our shores.

Greed. Our absolute faith in the markets, fed by Wall Street, combined with the declawing of our regulators to undermine our financial system. Too many Americans rushed out to buy houses they couldn't afford. And too many Americans went bounding off to the local Best Buy to pick up—on credit—giant flat-screen televisions (so big the TVs wouldn't even fit in the shopping cart) that they couldn't afford either.

Self-interest. The auto industry disintegrated while management and labor tangoed from one bad contract to the next, ignoring their customers and their competition, aided and abetted by their respective politicians.

Deferral of responsibility. Our power grid needs an upgrade and our bridges are falling down because we have not mustered the political and popular will to fix them. New Orleans drowned because authorities failed to act before Katrina busted the inadequate levees.

It was almost as if we as a nation said in previous decades, "Why do today what we can put off until the first decade of the 21st century?" We didn't rise to those challenges. What we have just lived through, then, was the chickens coming home to roost.

Take the vexing and costly war we are waging against al Qaeda and its ilk. This is a conflict that was barely on the radar in the 1990s—which is exactly the problem. By most accounts, Osama bin Laden founded his organization sometime between 1988 and 1990. The U.S. itself helped create this loathsome band, in part, by funding the mujahadeen, who fought the Soviets in Afghanistan in the 1980s and provided much of the training for bin Laden's foot soldiers. But our friendly freedom fighters turned into foes. In 1992, al Qaeda bombed a hotel in Yemen, hoping to kill American Marines bound for Somalia. Then came the first World Trade Center bombing, in 1993. Three years later the Khobar Towers bombing in Saudi Arabia killed 19 U.S. Air Force personnel. In 1996 and 1998, bin Laden issued fatwas calling for Muslims to rise up and kill Americans. Making good on bin Laden's word, al Qaeda blew up U.S. embassies in Kenya and Tanzania in synchronized attacks on Aug. 7, 1998, killing almost 300, including 12 Americans. In October 2000 terrorists struck again, bombing the destroyer

U.S.S. *Cole* in Yemen and killing 17 service members.

After all that, should 9/11 have been a surprise? There were those who saw what was coming, most notably FBI agent John O'Neill, who perished during the attack on the World Trade Center and whose story is eloquently told in Lawrence Wright's masterly book *The Looming Tower: Al-Qaeda and the Road to 9/11*. Time and time again O'Neill warned his superiors that al Qaeda was readying a big strike, only to be marginalized, causing him to leave the bureau.

Another prescient voice was that of Harvard professor Samuel Huntington, whose book *The Clash of Civilizations and the Remaking of World Order* suggested that culture and religion would be the sources of conflict in the post–Cold War world. Huntington didn't limit this to war between the West and Islam, though he did single out "Islamic civilization" as potentially having significant friction points with the West because of its burgeoning population and the rise of religious fundamentalism.

Our economic narcissism was certainly the culprit in the devastation wrought by financial markets, which have subjected us to an increasingly frequent series of crashes, frauds, and recessions. To a great degree this was brought about by a lethal combination of irresponsible deregulation and accommodating monetary policies instituted by the Federal Reserve. Bankers and financial engineers had an unsupervised free-market free-for-all just as the increased complexity of financial products—e.g., derivatives—screamed out for greater regulation, or at least supervision. Enron, for instance, was a bastard child of a deregulated utilities industry and mind-bending financial alchemy.

Historian H.W. Brands of the University of Texas points to the demise of the Glass-Steagall Act in 1999 as an unfortunate tipping point of deregulation. Glass-Steagall, passed in 1933, separated investment banking and plain-vanilla banking, which some experts argued made markets safer. (Certain restrictions of Glass-Steagall were repealed to allow the merger of Citicorp and Travelers. Let's just say that didn't end well.) "That was the single moment when the seeds for the bad stuff were planted," says Brands. "There was a belief that technology, the Internet, and financial instruments had changed things, and the ones selling this idea and these instruments were making a lot of money."

Another proximate cause were new loosey-goosey borrowing rules (if they can be called that) that allowed the likes of Bear Stearns and Lehman to pile $30 of debt onto each $1 of capital. The chief executives of those firms argued vociferously for the right to greater leverage and vociferously against regulating derivatives because, they claimed, unfettered markets were more efficient. Yes, it was the unfettered use of leverage and derivatives that destroyed their companies and wreaked havoc on the rest of us.

Companies go belly-up all the time, but in this decade there was an inordinate number of bankruptcies. The creative destruction of the Internet had a part in this. While the web opened up new worlds and created thousands of jobs at Amazon, Google, and the like, it displaced workers at travel and government agencies, at newspapers and magazines, and at stores like Circuit City and Tower Records—traditional distribution points for services, information, and goods. Economists call that disintermediation.

But when we're talking about auto giants GM and Chrysler, both of which imploded after years of complicity and ineptitude by GM management and the United Auto Workers (UAW), it's more like disintegration. The UAW organized both GM and Chrysler in early 1937; Henry Ford famously held out four more years. For decades, particularly under the leadership of Walter Reuther, who headed it from 1946 until his death in 1970, the union was able to win concessions from the automakers, bringing its members into the middle class. As long as demand for autos grew in the post–World War II halcyon days, relations between the unions and the automakers were basically quiescent.

And therein lies the problem. For years the UAW and the Big Three—now dwindled to the Detroit Three— operated an unholy alliance. Management would pile on wage hikes and perks, and in return (wink, wink) the union would keep the peace—i.e., rule out strikes. Both sides must have realized that the amount being paid to workers was unsustainable, particularly if the industry hit any downdrafts, which happened with increasing frequency starting with the 1973 OPEC oil embargo.

Just as embarrassing was the colossal ineptitude of the big car companies: Ugly, low-quality cars with shameful gas mileage. Layers of redundant management that relied on amateurish financial controls. Insular thinking reinforced by decades of outsize market share. It was as if Detroit had drawn a road map for Toyota and Honda. And the Japanese drove right in, decimating the U.S. companies. In 1979, GM's U.S. employment peaked at 618,365. Today it's at 75,000 and falling fast. GM's U.S. market share, once about 50%, has fallen to about 20%. True, the quality and efficiency of American cars have improved dramatically, but it may be too late.

IV

Not Just Acts of God

AND WHAT ABOUT THE HURRICANE KATRINA DEBACLE?
An act of God, right? Not really. When the storm raced
toward New Orleans in late August 2005, scientists at
the National Oceanic and Atmospheric Administration
feared the worst. For years they had been warning the
U.S. Army Corps of Engineers, which oversaw the city's
350 miles of levees, that its system was inadequate.
The scientists wanted the Corps to revise the Standard
Project Hurricane, a model that determines how exten-

New Orleans, August 2005 *An aerial photograph shows devastation
caused by high winds and flooding after the historic city's levees broke.*

sive the levees should be. For instance, the Corps did not consider the tendency of the soil to sink over time, and it also excluded the possibility of a highly powerful storm hitting the city because it was unlikely—a position that violates sophisticated principles of statistics and just plain common sense.

On Nov. 18, 2009, a federal judge ruled that the Corps was directly responsible for flooding in St. Bernard Parish and the Lower Ninth Ward. "The Corps' lassitude and failure to fulfill its duties resulted in a catastrophic loss of human life and property in unprecedented proportions," the judge said.

Apart from the failings of the Corps of Engineers, mismanagement by the local levee boards contributed to substandard levees. Hurricane Katrina wasn't even as bad a storm as had been feared—but the levees weren't as good as had been hoped. Some fact-based decision-making could have saved hundreds of lives and billions of dollars. Here, too, years and years of complacency were the rule, not the exception. The price was paid this decade.

It's also worth considering the effect that climate

change—i.e., global warming—might have had in creating Katrina. There are those who suggest that heightened levels of man-made greenhouse gases have altered our climate in such a way as to produce more extreme weather patterns. And, of course, 2005 was a record year for hurricanes, which seemed to give credence to that theory. Since then, hurricane seasons have been relatively calmer, though four years is way too brief a period for any sort of scientific measure.

The larger point, however—that global warming does exist, that it is created by human behavior, and that it is harmful to our planet—is now considered irrefutable by mainstream scientists, politicians, and even businessmen. This comes after years of denial by shortsighted individuals who were more interested in hitting quarterly profit targets and by the people who would cozy up to them. Environmental neglect has sadly been another hallmark of our society in the years leading up to this past decade, and it has produced dire consequences.

Even if we leave aside climate change as a determinant for the national nightmare that was Katrina, we

are still left with neglect and deteriorating infrastructure as proximate causes. Unfortunately the effect of those two trends extends far beyond the Crescent City.

At 6:05 p.m. on Aug. 1, 2007, the Minneapolis I-35 W bridge spanning the Mississippi River collapsed, killing 13 and injuring 145. The National Transportation Safety Board later cited a design flaw as the cause, but the bridge had been classified as "structurally deficient" since 1991, according to a Highway Accident Report. The bridge, which opened some four decades ago in 1967, was scheduled to be replaced in 2020.

How many other bridges, highways, and dams are deathtraps in waiting? No one knows, but you can't help wondering whether squeezed maintenance budgets are making our country less safe.

A 2005 report card on American infrastructure by the American Society of Civil Engineers (which gave mostly C's and D's) estimated that the U.S. needed to spend $1.6 trillion to bring our roads, highways, bridges, and dams into good shape. Sure, the engineers are looking for work, but know that the U.S. spends only 2.4% of its

gross domestic product on infrastructure, as opposed to 5% in Europe and 9% in China. Here again, why should a politician spend money today to fix something that won't collapse until tomorrow? Especially if he or she could get reelected by cutting taxes instead.

V.

Starting Over

IF WE ARE NOW WATCHING THE SUN SET ON A DECADE
from hell, does it naturally follow that the next decade will be all good and glory? Of course not. And
yet there are some hopeful signs. We have seen the
destructiveness of deferral and neglect on infrastructure, national and global politics, financial markets,
and corporate governance, and I think it's safe to say
that the awareness of that danger is much higher
now. Maybe that is why, for the first time, a national

San Francisco Bay Bridge, 2009 *Bay Area commuters cross a newly
added section of roadway after a crack in a steel link had closed the span.*

health-care bill actually has a chance to become law.

Truly reversing some of the trends that have been vexing our society over the past several decades, and which came to a head in the first part of this century, requires a new perspective. To see how this might come about, or in some cases is already changing, let's look back to the bullet points (from hell) in Chapter III, "What Went Wrong," as a guide.

Neglect. A critical manifestation of our neglect was that our inward-looking culture didn't heed warnings about Islamic terrorism. Well, we are certainly more outward-looking today. But perhaps we are too outward-looking, or at least outward-looking in the wrong way. Our armies are spread thin in Iraq and Afghanistan as we yet again try to play policeman to the world. How many times must we go down this potholed road before we realize it offers no long-term solutions and is fraught with negative unintended consequences?

Peter Bishop, coordinator of the graduate program in future studies at the University of Houston, argues persuasively that terrorism is a "low-grade fever" that will be around for a long time. "Vigilance is required, but not necessarily the kind of aggressive offense that we've gone after," he says. Bishop believes a law-enforcement approach to terrorism would have been preferable to our current blanket military strategy: "Europeans treat terror as a crime, and they go after people, put them on trial, and put them in jail. That's what they did with the IRA, and ultimately beat that down, and what Spain did."

By the way, this is exactly what the U.S. has done domestically to fight terror, with great success. Overseas is where we should look to change our methods, and that means fewer mass deployments and more strategic engagement, spycraft, and hearts-and-minds stuff. Net-net, if we want to engage in fact-based decision-making, a protracted show of force, while playing to the strength of the U.S., is not necessarily the best response.

Greed. We will never eliminate greed, of course, and a certain amount of it may even be necessary—as Gordon Gekko famously says in the movie *Wall Street*, "Greed … is good." Consider the role of greed in innovation. Part of what motivates an entrepreneur is self-interest. Without the hope of getting rich, many dreamers would remain just that, dreamers.

Certainly, though, unchecked greed is unwelcome and ruinous. Recent developments in our housing markets and on Wall Street make that plainly obvious. Politicians and economists have alluded to this when they describe the "animal spirits" within us and how they cannot be tamed—but could be tempered.

Chief White House economic adviser Larry Summers has suggested that we apply the same mindset to our financial markets that we have to highway safety, and cites one of Daniel Patrick Moynihan's public-policy proposals to improve highways and cars in the 1950s. Moynihan's insight: Americans will always drive too fast, yet we can mitigate some of the risk to life by requiring seatbelts, imposing speed limits, and installing guardrails and shatterproof glass. And we did do that, and death rates on our roads dropped substantially.

Summers' point, in terms of our financial markets, was that just because we can't rid human beings of excessive greed doesn't mean we shouldn't work to curb its effects. Doing so would, of course, require more regulation and oversight. But who, after the events of the past two years, would argue against that?

How do we fix Wall Street? By facing the music now. Toughen borrowing requirements by banks. Increase oversight, especially in regulating derivatives. Perhaps enact a 21st-century version of Glass-Steagall. And don't allow any institution to become too big to fail.

Does that mean some countries may get ahead of us in terms of financial innovation? Sure, but so what? For much of this decade, both England and Iceland were considered friendlier to capital markets than the U.S. England is now threadbare; Iceland is bankrupt.

Self-interest. Exhibit A is our auto industry, in particular GM, now just a shadow of its former self-righteous self, thanks to decades of shortsightedness. Today the prognoses for GM, Chrysler, and Ford range from the jury's out, to dire, to hopeful, respectively. At the very least there is awareness that the reset button has been hit, and that these companies must be reconceived or they will surely fail. Chrysler in particular must act fast to show drivers that it has an appealing new line of cars and trucks. GM, now looking for its third CEO in less than a year, must rid itself once and for all of its insularity and implement real financial controls. Ford—which, unlike its two wheezing kin, did not file for bankruptcy or take a government bail-out—must still prove it is a sustainable automaker.

There are lessons to be learned here from the fast-est-growing (yes, growing) car company in the world: Hyundai. This Korean automaker is winning by being hyper-aggressive, super-lean, and flexible, and obsessing over the details. Then there's the "pay attention to your customers" part. The company engendered massive good will when it rolled out a promotion where if you bought a Hyundai and later lost your job, you could return the vehicle and get your cash back. Only 100 or so customers did, but the publicity made up for the loss 1,000-fold. Want proof that all of this works? Hyundai's net profits are expected to soar 40% this year.

Deferral of responsibility. As noted previously, year after year, decade after decade, we have underinvested in infrastructure. Sadly, even given the promise of Washington's stimulus package, we are still lagging behind when it comes to building and rebuilding the inner workings of our country.

Spending on infrastructure is expected to decline 4.3% in 2009, according to the U.S. Infrastructure Market Analysis from IHS Global Insight's Construction Service. How is that possible, given government spending programs? First, because spending on public works projects comes not only from federal programs but also from state and local budgets, and because of depleted local coffers, states and towns have slashed spending on roads and bridges.

Second, federal spending has been mostly talk and no action. Economists will tell you it's mega-projects like Hoover Dam or Boston's Big Dig that really jump-start growth, and right now there is a paucity of such programs. President Obama has earmarked just $80 billion of his almost $800 billion stimulus package for big-ticket projects, and most of that has been deferred. Really, the only biggie on the drawing board is a giant computer system to digitize medical records. It might work, it might not—but it's hardly the next Golden Gate Bridge. Meanwhile only some $8 billion in stimulus money has been allotted to new rail systems. A pittance, especially considering that China will spend $300 billion on high-speed rail during the next decade. Will we have the political and economic fortitude to crank up spending? We had better.

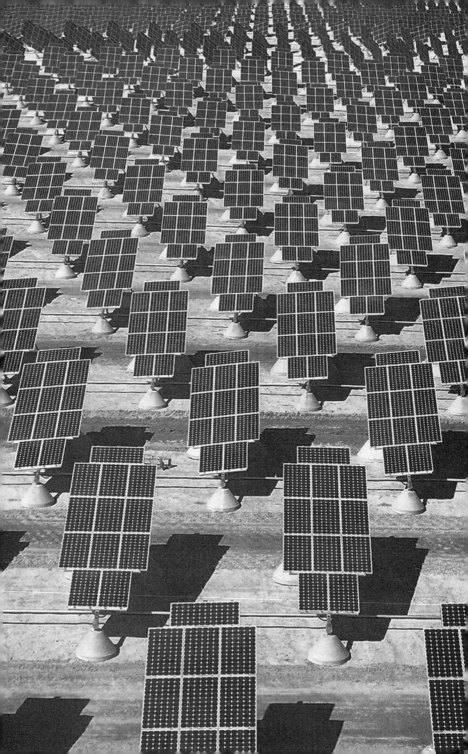

VI.
The Promise

EVEN ASSUMING WE'VE LEARNED ENOUGH FROM THE past to correct the bad habits we have fallen into, is there anything we can point to that would signal a real shift from our current trajectory? I'm talking about a game-changing geopolitical or economic development such as the end of the Cold War or the rise of China. By definition these kinds of events may be impossible to see, but they are out there. Deny them at your peril. It's also important to remember that there are natural

Renewable energy *Some of the 70,000 solar panels that are generating electricity for Nellis Air Force Base outside Las Vegas*

---

cycles in history. Unless you believe that this country is in the throes of a deep and permanent decline, there's no question that we will rebound. "Usually when you've had a really bad decade like this one, the next decade turns out to be much better for investors," says Richard Sylla, a professor of economics at New York University's Stern School of Business. "Probably 10 years from now, people who are investing today are going to have fairly nice returns." Over time, stocks have averaged a total return of about 9%. Remember, stocks were down 1.2% a year this decade, after being up 18.2% a year in the 1990s. Returns always revert to the mean.

And also recall that the stock market usually mirrors political and economic trends. When the future appears stable and certain, the market moves up. When unexpectedly positive events occur, like the Internet boom in the 1990s, stocks produce above-average returns. This decade the surprises were mostly negative, which drove the market lower. At some point, unanticipated positive developments will again drive the market higher. What could they be? If the answer to that were simple, I'd be on a beach sipping Pernod by now.

But it's not impossible to make some educated guesses. At some point a sustained easing of tensions between the West and radical Islam will probably occur, and the global peace dividend and sense of relief that ensues could be most powerful. But more than that, and using the U.S. as a starting point, what are the likely stepping-off points to significant growth opportunities?

You often hear pundits bemoaning the demise of manufacturing in the U.S. What these folks are really talking about are low-end goods such as plastic lawn furniture and some apparel, as well as finished commodity products like steel and copper tubing. (There are exceptions here, of course.) Further up the product chain—meaning the more sophisticated a product is—we are still very much in the game. And that's no small thing. The U.S. leads the world in the creation of what is generally referred to as software or intellectual property, which is lucky for us, since that's the most profitable and fastest-growing slice of the global economy. Will that be enough to lift up everyone in America? No. But we must recognize and leverage this promise to maximize its effect. "The future is already here," says Arthur Harkins, faculty director for innovation studies at the University of Minnesota, paraphrasing cyberpunk novelist William Gibson. "It's just not evenly allocated."

The promise of software carries hundreds of billions of dollars of value and cuts across all kinds of businesses. It does require a highly skilled and educated workforce, but that's another positive, because we happen to have the greatest collection of universities on the planet. And then there's the continued promise of the U.S. economy. The World Bank ranks the U.S. fourth in its Ease of Doing Business index, trailing only Singapore, New Zealand, and Hong Kong out of 183 countries. What that really means is that we are the best large economy in the world in which to do business. That is an unimaginably huge advantage. (Countries are ranked on 10 factors, such as how easy it is to start a business, whether credit is available, whether contracts can be enforced, etc.)

Before I get into the biggest opportunities in software, let's put aside what had until recently been a significant segment here, and that is financial innovation, meaning the creation of complex, computerized financial instruments such as derivatives. The good news is that America was a world leader in this field; the bad news is that it almost destroyed the global economy. There is still upside in the derivatives business, but buyers are rightly skeptical, and further regulation is probably called for.

More promising are a slew of other fields, such as entertainment, which along with aircraft (read: Boeing, and think of all the software in those aircraft) is one of this country's largest exports. Demand for our TV shows, movies, games, and apps will grow much faster than that for other businesses. And then there is the main event itself, or what we have traditionally called software. Apple, Microsoft, Oracle, eBay, Amazon, Adobe, Yahoo, Google, AOL, and Facebook, not to mention Twitter and LinkedIn, are all software companies and employ hundreds of thousands of people. And many are adding jobs even in this economy. They are companies with global reach, and many of them have sizable and sustainable competitive positions.

Consider just one sliver of this business: smartphones. The industry leader on the innovation side, Apple with its iPhone, is creating a business—never mind a cultural revolution—through this product's apps function, which allows small developers to create an unlimited number of software programs—100,000 and counting—that enable us to shop for cool shoes, track what's left of our 401(k)s, find a place to eat Korean food, and play games like FarmVille anywhere, anytime. The other players, like Google, Palm, and Canada's RIM (its product is the BlackBerry), are scrambling to keep up. The takeaway here: This is a global business that is exploding yet is very much centered in North America.

The U.S. will also benefit greatly from selling software know-how into manufacturing and engineering, including everything from cars to appliances to agriculture and beyond. "I tend to think of technologies as waves," says Peter Bishop of the University of Houston. "My candidate for the next wave is biotechnology." Bishop believes that "we will finally get our arms around how to manipulate code for DNA, create synthetic organisms as a platform, and then design how we want those things to work for food, for energy, and of course then extending it into human health."

And the holy grail of this century, finding and optimizing energy sources beyond oil, gas, and coal, will naturally entail technological expertise—think batteries, as well as solar, wind, and geothermal—and likely even biotechnological prowess. Bishop gives an example: "Biofuels, particularly algae, are probably going to really boom. I think we're going to see large algae farms, where you need three resources—water, sunlight, and a source of carbon dioxide, because grabbing it out of the air isn't efficient enough. So you'll put an algae farm next to a coal plant or a natural gas plant and try to pump CO_2 into the algae and then turn the algae into a biofuel."

Growth will come from unlikely sources too. The mushrooming Hispanic population in the U.S. will make for myriad new business opportunities. Water may become scarce—certainly a negative—but a rational distribution system will prove to be highly valuable. Legal medical marijuana is already a multimillion-dollar business. And then there are the really big problems, which could be really big opportunities. "If you say we've got this huge crumbling infrastructure in Africa —maybe the world gets together and says we really need to do something about this," postulates Bishop.

"We beat back fascism in the 1940s and created tre-
mendously prosperous societies from the ruins of those
countries. We beat back communism in the 1980s. So
today the problems of poverty and lack of resources are
huge, but that might mean that the world gets together
and says, 'We can fix this.'"

And don't forget global warming. Futurist Jamais
Cascio speaks of geo-engineering as a possible way to
moderate the worst effects of climate change. "The one
that gets the most attention is the proposal to pump
megatons of sulfur dioxide particles into the upper
stratosphere," he says. It emulates one of the aspects
of a giant volcanic eruption by "cooling the planet for
a short period of time." Sound far-fetched? Sure, but so
do most transformational ideas, at least initially.

The point is, if we were too positive heading into the
2000s, we are almost certainly too negative heading
into the next decade. But that's not such a bad thing.
It means we will be collectively reluctant to lard on
massive debts. It means we will be wary when some
mortgage man tries to sell us an exotic loan predicated
on our house's doubling in value. It means we will see

"financial innovation" for what it often is: an oxymoron. And most important, it means we will take more seriously our responsibility to address problems now rather than later.

There is no guarantee that the next decade (get ready for the Teens!) will be any better than this one. It's likely that China will continue to grow faster than the U.S., and we may continue to see our global dominance erode. But very significantly, we still hold many of the world's trump cards. We still have the world's strongest military, which means that we can and must take the initiative in maintaining order and crafting peace. We are the leaders in technological innovation. And we are still the nation that most others emulate. If we remember those points and avoid the easy outs of deferral and neglect, then the next decade should be a helluva lot better than the last one.

Acknowledgments

I am very grateful for the assistance and contributions of the following people. Without them it would not have been possible to produce this book. Beth Kowitt, *Fortune* writer-reporter, handled reporting. Romesh Ratnesar, *Time* deputy managing editor, edited the book. Hillary Raskin created a comprehensive and intelligent collection of photos. D.W. Pine, *Time* deputy art director, devised a simple, elegant design. Lonnie Vargas, our production manager, was the engine moving things along, while Suzanne Janso took care of printing arrangements. *Fortune* copy chief Carol Gwinn did the copy editing, aided by Jonathan Brown and Edith Fried. And of course, my thanks to Rick Stengel, *Time* managing editor, who pushed to make this book happen and contributed the introduction, and to the folks at Time Inc. Home Entertainment who pulled all the strings that made it work: Joy Butts, assistant publishing director, and Michela Wilde, associate brand manager.

I also wish to acknowledge the efforts of Ratu Kamlani, *Time* assistant managing editor; Cindy Connolly of the Time Inc. legal department; Rick Prue, editorial operations director; Daniel Kile, *Time* associate director of public relations; Sydney Webber, director of trade marketing at Time Inc. Home Entertainment; Michelle Gallero, the prepress manager; and for securing promotions, Tammy Henault, Jennifer Levin, April Schwab, Allison Ehrmann, and Steven Vasiliades. Lastly, my thanks to Richard Fraiman, president and publisher of Time Inc. Home Entertainment, for publishing this book.

Photo Credits

TIMELINE OF EVENTS

Page 16: Stuart Ramsom—AP; *page 18:* Doug Mills—AP;
page 20: CNN via Getty Images;
page 22: Robert Giroux—Getty Images;
page 24: AP Photo/Courtesy of *The New Yorker*;
page 26: Mehdi Ghassemi—ISNA/Reuters;
page 28: Iraqi TV/AP Photo; *page 30:* Hector Emanuel;
page 32: Jonathan Ernst—Reuters; *page 34:* David Karp—AP

CHAPTERS

Page 38: Carmen Taylor—AP Photos; *page 44:* Anthony Suau;
page 52: Bryan Denton—Corbis; *page 62:* Vincent LaForet—
Reuters/Pool; *page 68:* Justin Sullivan—Getty Images;
page 76: Airman 1st Class Nadine Y. Barclay—U.S. Air Force/Reuters

About the Author

Andy Serwer is the managing editor of *Fortune*, a global leader in business journalism known for its unrivaled access to industry executives, with a worldwide circulation of more than 1 million. In addition to covering Wall Street, investing, information technology, and entertainment for the magazine, Serwer has written a provocative column as well as major cover stories on everything from the young Michael Dell to Michael Price ("The Toughest S.O.B. on Wall Street") to the first look inside the financial and philanthropic workings of America's richest family, the Waltons.